PRAYERS
OF THOSE
WHO MOURN

LITURGY TRAINING PUBLICATIONS

In paradisum deducant te angeli:
in tuo adventu suscipiant te martyres,
et perducant te in civitatem sanctam Jerusalem.
Chorus angelorum suscipiat,
et cum Lazaro quondam paupere aeternam
habeas requiem.

May the angels lead you into paradise;
may the martyrs come to welcome you
and take you to the holy city,
the new and eternal Jerusalem.
May the choir of angels welcome you,
and where Lazarus is poor no longer
may you find eternal rest.

ACKNOWLEDGMENTS

Excerpts from the *Order of Christian Funerals,* copyright © 1989, International Committee on English in the Liturgy, Inc.

The translation of the psalms copyright © 1994, International Committee on English in the Liturgy, Inc.

Scripture passages (except pages 3–5) are taken from the New Revised Standard Version, copyright © 1989, Division of Christian Education, National Council of the Churches of Christ in the United States of America.

Scripture passages on pages 3–5 from the New American Bible with Revised New Testament, copyright © 1986 by the Confraternity of Christian Doctrine, Washington, DC, are used by permission of the copyright owner. All rights reserved.

Excerpts from *The Book of Common Prayer.* Published by the Seabury Press, New York.

"We hold the death," by David Haas, copyright © 1983; English translation of the Salve Regina by John C. Selner, copyright © 1954, GIA.

"Jesus remember me," by Jacques Berthier, copyright © 1981, Les Presses de Taize, GIA Publications, Inc., agent.

"Jesus, savior of the world," by William Storey, from *Pray Like This,* copyright © 1963 by Fides Publishers.

"Let us pray for ourselves," by Huub Oosterhuis, from *Your Word is Near,* copyright © 1968 by The Missionary Society of St. Paul the Apostle in the state of New York.

"Contakion of the Departed," anonymous. From *The Harper Book of Christian Poetry,* selected and introduced by Anthony S. Mercatante. Copyright © 1972, Anthony S. Mercatante. Published by Harper and Row Publishers, Inc. Used with permission.

"The embalming of the corpse," by Augustine, from *Roman Breviary in English,* (Autumn), edited by Msgr. Joseph A. Nelson. Copyright © 1950, Benzinger Publishing Co., Mission Hills CA.

This book was compiled, and the introductions written by David Philippart, with editorial assistance from Pedro A. Vélez. It was designed by Kerry Perlmutter and Anna Manhart and typeset in Galliard by Karen Mitchell. Andy Manhart did the artwork. *Prayers of Those Who Mourn* was printed in the United States of America by Salsedo Press, Inc.

Other prayerbooks in this series include *Prayers of the Sick, Rites of the Sick,* and *Prayers of the Dying.* For further reflection on the mystery of death, see *Death: A Sourcebook,* available from LTP.

Library of Congress Catalog Card Number 95-81606
ISBN 1-56854-132-5
MOURNR

BLEST ARE THEY WHO MOURN

In a society that tries so hard to avoid and escape and deny death, we Christians face it—not necessarily willingly or happily—but faithfully, in hope, and with love for the dead one and for each other. In fact, the rituals that we do in the face of death lead us to embrace death slowly, in the words of Francis of Assisi, as our sister. And so we mourn, not to be maudlin. Rather, in words, tunes, gestures and rites we wrestle—we wrestle *together*—with the paschal mystery: To be born, one first must die.

We have the courage to wrestle together with mystery because Jesus passed first through death to life, showing us the way. Each year we celebrate the great and holy Triduum—the three days of Christ's passion, death and burial, and resurrection. Is it any wonder that when any one of us makes our own passover, that the church marks it with three stations? The Order of Christian Funerals provides for each baptized believer and catechumen a trinity of rites: the vigil, the funeral liturgy and the rite of committal. What happened to Jesus happens to us.

This book will assist you through the other times, the hours before and between and after the three stations of the Christian funeral rite. The scriptures are silent about this: What did the disciples do after they buried Jesus and before the women found him risen? We can only imagine that they kept watch in silence and in song, with words and working through worry, reaching for promise and for peace. May this book help you do likewise.

GATHERING IN THE
PRESENCE OF THE BODY

We face death squarely when we gather in the presence of the body of our loved one for the first time. Jesus knew such pain: He wept when he arrived at Lazarus' tomb. Mary knew such pain: After watching her son die on the cross, she cradled his lifeless body in her arms.

Jesus and Mary assure us: God is with us in our sorrow. We turn to God in prayer:

The Sign of the Cross
A Verse from Scripture
Sprinkling the Body with Holy Water
A Psalm
The Lord's Prayer
Concluding Prayer
Blessing

A priest, deacon or other minister from the parish may lead us, as may a family member or friend.

We Sign Ourselves with the Cross

We Listen to God's Word

One person reads aloud or recites from memory one of the following or another brief verse:

My brothers and sisters, Jesus says:
"Come to me, all you who labor and are burdened, and I will give you rest. Take my yoke upon you and learn from me, for I am meek and humble of heart; and you will find rest for yourselves. For my yoke is easy, and my burden light."

— *Matthew 11:28 – 30*

Or:

My brothers and sisters, Jesus says:
"Do not let your hearts be troubled. You have faith in God; have faith also in me. In my Father's house there are many dwelling places. If there were not, would I have told you that I am going to prepare a place for you? And if I go and prepare a place for you, I will come back again

and take you to myself, so that where I am you
also may be."

—John 14:1–3

We pause for silent prayer.

We Sprinkle the Body with Holy Water

*To remember baptism, the minister sprinkles
the body with holy water and says one of the
following:*

The Lord is our shepherd
and leads us to streams of living water.

Or:
Let this water call to mind
   our baptism into Christ,
who by his death and resurrection
   has redeemed us.

Or:
The Lord God lives in his holy temple
   yet abides in our midst.

Since in baptism *Name* became God's temple
and the Spirit of God lived in *him/her*,
with reverence we bless *his/her* mortal body.

We Pray A Psalm

*We sing or say a psalm, such as the psalm on
page 28, Psalm 23 or the one below:*

**R: I will walk in the presence
of the Lord,
in the land of the living.**

How gracious is the Lord, and just;
our God has compassion.
The Lord protects the simple hearts;
I was helpless so he saved me.
I trusted, even when I said:
"I am sorely afflicted,"
and when I said in my alarm:
"No man can be trusted."

O precious in the eyes of the Lord
is the death of his faithful.

Your servant, Lord, your servant am I;
you have loosened my bonds.

—Psalm 116

We Pray the Lord's Prayer

The minister says one of the following:

With God there is mercy and fullness of redemption; let us pray as Jesus taught us . . .

Or:

Let us pray for the coming of the kingdom as Jesus taught us . . .

We Conclude

The minister says a closing prayer, such as the one on page 25 or 44. Then the minister says:

Blessed are those who have died in the Lord; let them rest from their labors for their good deeds go with them.

All may sign the forehead of the deceased with the cross as the following prayer is said:

Minister: Eternal rest grant unto *him/her,* O Lord.

All: **And let perpetual light shine upon *him/her.***

Minister: May *he/she* rest in peace.

All: **Amen.**

Minister: May *his/her* soul and the souls of all the faithful departed,
through the mercy of God, rest in peace.

All: **Amen.**

If a priest or deacon, the minister gives the usual blessing. All sign themselves with the cross. A minister who is a lay person says:

May the love of God
and the peace of the Lord Jesus Christ
bless us and console us
and gently wipe every tear from our eyes:

in the name of the Father,
and of the Son, and of the Holy Spirit.

    All: **Amen.**

*All may sing this song to the tune of Tallis' canon
or "Praise God from whom all blessings flow":*

May saints and angels lead you on,
Escorting you where Christ has gone.
Now Christ has called you, come to him,
Who sits above the seraphim.

Come to the peace of Abraham
And to the supper of the Lamb:
Come to the glory of the blessed,
And to perpetual light and rest.

*This song may be used all throughout the wake, to
greet the body when mourners first gather and to
take leave of the body each night.*

KEEPING WATCH

The first part of a Christian funeral, the principal rite of the wake, is the vigil, when ministers and members of the parish gather with family and friends of the deceased for introductory rites, the liturgy of the word, prayers of intercession and a concluding rite.

Family members and friends may want to pray together at other times as they keep watch with the body. The following prayers will help, but others—particularly ones that all know by heart or that were important to the deceased—may be used as well. Praying the sorrowful mysteries of the rosary is a good example. Singing together is not only a good way of thanking God for the life of the deceased and seeking mercy—it is a healthy way of expressing grief.

WAKE PRAYERS

*Sing this song to its own tune or that of "Praise
God from whom all blessings flow." Other songs are
on pages 8, 13, 14, 24, 29, 45 and 52.*

I know that my Redeemer lives!
What joy the blest assurance gives!
He lives, he lives who once was dead;
He lives, my ever-living head!

He lives to grant me rich supply;
He lives to guide me with his eye;
He lives to comfort me when faint;
He lives to hear my soul's complaint.

He lives to silence all my fears;
He lives to wipe away my tears;
He lives to calm my troubled heart;
He lives all blessings to impart.

He lives, all glory to the Name!
He lives, my Savior, still the same,

What joy the blest assurance gives:
I know that my Redeemer lives!

—Based on Job 19:25, Samuel Medley, alt.

Blessed be the God and Father of our Lord Jesus
Christ, who in great mercy has given us a new
birth into living hope through the resurrection
of Jesus Christ from the dead!

Amen!

Blest are those who mourn.

They shall be comforted.

*Scriptures may be read from pages 29, 44, 51
and 57. Pause between readings, or sing psalms or
hymns. Then read the following scriptures.*

Do you not know that all of us who have been
baptized into Christ Jesus were baptized into his
death? Therefore we have been buried with
him by baptism into death, so that, just as Christ

was raised from the dead by the glory of the Father, so we too might walk in newness of life.

For if we have been united with him in a death like his, we will certainly be united with him in a resurrection like his. We know that our old self was crucified with him so that the body of sin might be destroyed, and we might no longer be enslaved to sin. For whoever has died is freed from sin. But if we have died with Christ, we believe that we will also live with him. So you also must consider yourselves dead to sin and alive to God in Christ Jesus.

—*Romans 6:3–8, 11*

We hold the death of the Lord
    deep in our hearts.
Living, now we remain with Jesus the Christ.

—*David Haas*

One of the criminals who were hanged there kept deriding Jesus and saying, "Are you not the

Messiah? Save yourself and us!" But the other
rebuked him, saying, "Do you not fear
God, since you are under the same sentence of
condemnation? And we indeed have been
condemned justly, for we are getting what we
deserve for our deeds, but this man has done
nothing wrong." Then he said, "Jesus, remember me when you come into your kingdom."
He replied, "Truly I tell you, today you will be
with me in paradise." It was . . . about noon and
darkness came over the whole land.

— *Luke 23:39-44*

Jesus, remember me,
    when you come into your kingdom.

Jesus, remember me,
    when you come into your kingdom.

— *Jacques Berthier*

Jesus, savior of the world
    Grant *him/her* eternal rest.

Jesus, good shepherd of the flock
	Grant *him/her* eternal rest.
Jesus, the way, the truth, the life
	Grant *him/her* eternal rest.
Jesus, the first fruits of those who have fallen
	asleep in death
	Grant *him/her* eternal rest.
Jesus, the same yesterday, today and forever
	Grant *him/her* eternal rest.
Jesus, who shall come again in glory to judge the
	living and the dead
	Grant *him/her* eternal rest.

Let us pray for ourselves,
[who are severely tested by this death,]
that we do not try to minimize this loss
or seek to escape from it
and also that we do not brood over it
so that it overwhelms us
and isolates us from others.
May God grant us
	new courage and confidence to face life.
Let us pray for those who go on blindly,

unable to overcome their sorrow,
that they may be saved from despair
for God's sake and for the sake of their dead
that God, even in silence, may comfort them
and bear their burden with them.

— *Huub Oosterhuis*

All pray silently for a time. Then all pray the Lord's Prayer.

May the memory of *Name*,
   [who is worthy of praise]
remain with us forever.

   Amen.

May God bless us, the Father, the Son and the Holy Spirit.

   Amen.

Hail, Queen of heaven,
hail our Mother compassionate,
True life and comfort
     and our hope, we greet you!
To you we exiles,
children of Eve, raise our voices.
We send up sighs to you,
as mourning and weeping,
we pass through this vale of sorrow.
Then turn to us,
O most gracious Woman,
those eyes of yours,
so full of love and tenderness,
so full of pity.
And grant us after these, our days of lonely exile,
the sight
of your blest Son and Lord,
Christ Jesus.
O gentle, O loving, O holy
sweet Virgin Mary.

    —*Translated by John C. Selner*

Prayers Before Taking the Body to Church

When it is time to take the body to church, the following order of prayer is used. It may be led by a parish minister, funeral director, family member or friend:

Minister:

Dear friends in Christ, in the name of Jesus and of his church, we gather to pray for *Name*, that God may bring *him/her* to everlasting peace and rest.

We share the pain of loss, but the promise of eternal life gives us hope. Let us comfort one another with these words:

You have died, and your life is hidden with Christ in God. When Christ your life appears, then you too will appear with him in glory.

— *Colossians 3:3 – 4*

Or:

If we have died with Christ, we believe that we shall also live with him. We know that Christ, raised from the dead, dies no more; death no longer has power over him.

—*Romans 6:8 – 9*

The minister continues:

Dear friends, our Lord comes to raise the dead and comforts us with the solace of his love. Let us praise the Lord Jesus Christ.

An assisting minister leads the litany:

Word of God, creator of the earth to which *Name* now returns: In baptism you called *him/her* to eternal life to praise your Father forever: Lord, have mercy.

All: Lord, have mercy!

Son of God, you raise up the just and clothe
them with the glory of your kingdom: Lord,
have mercy.

> *All:* **Lord, have mercy!**

Crucified Lord, you protect the soul of *Name* by
the power of your cross, and on the day of
your coming you will show mercy to all the faithful departed: Lord, have mercy.

> *All:* **Lord, have mercy!**

Judge of the living and the dead, at your voice
the tombs will open, and all the just who
sleep will rise and sing the glory of God: Lord,
have mercy.

> *All:* **Lord, have mercy!**

All praise to you, Jesus our Savior, death is
in your hands and all the living depend on you
alone: Lord, have mercy.

> *All:* **Lord, have mercy!**

Minister:

With faith and hope we pray to the Father in the words Jesus taught his disciples:

All: **Our Father . . .**

The minister says the following prayer or the ones found on pages 33-36 or 42:

God of all consolation,
open our hearts to your word,
so that, listening to it, we may comfort one
    another,
finding light in time of darkness
and faith in time of doubt.
We ask this through Christ our Lord.
Amen.

The minister invites all to pray silently while all is made ready for the procession to church. When all is ready, the minister says:

The Lord guards our coming in
    and our going out.
May God be with us today

as we make this last journey
with our *brother/sister.*

A song may be sung as the body is taken out of the
funeral home. It may be Psalm 22 or a song that
all know by heart, such as "Amazing grace."

IN THE DAYS AND WEEKS
AFTER BURIAL

There is a place of quiet rest,
    near to the heart of God;
A place where sin cannot molest,
    near to the heart of God.
  O Jesus, blest Redeemer,
    sent from the heart of God,
  Hold us who wait before Thee,
    near to the heart of God.
There is a place of comfort sweet,
    near to the heart of God;
A place where we our Savior can meet,
    near to the heart of God.
  O Jesus, blest Redeemer . . .
There is a place of full release,
    near to the heart of God;
A place where all is joy and peace,
    near to the heart of God.
  O Jesus, blest Redeemer . . .

  —*Cleland B. McAfee*

Father of mercies and God of all consolation,
you pursue us with untiring love

and dispel the shadow of death
with the bright dawn of life.

Comfort your family in their loss and sorrow.
Be our refuge and our strength, O Lord,
and lift us from the depths of grief
into the peace and light of your presence.

Your Son, our Lord Jesus Christ,
by dying has destroyed our death,
and by rising, restored our life.
Enable us therefore to press on toward him,
so that, after our earthly course is run,
he may reunite us with those we love,
when every tear will be wiped away.

We ask this through Christ our Lord.
Amen.

God of faithfulness,
in your wisdom you have called
      your servant *Name*
   out of this world;
release *him/her* from the bonds of sin,

and welcome *him/her* into your presence,
so that *he/she* may enjoy eternal light and peace
and be raised up in glory with all your saints.
We ask this through Christ our Lord.
Amen.

— *Order of Christian Funerals*

O Mother of Jesus,
at Golgotha you felt his pain;
your arms received his broken body.
Pray for us in our sorrowful days!

WHEN GRIEF IS TOO MUCH

From the depths I call to you,
Lord, hear my cry.
Catch the sound of my voice
raised up, pleading.

If you record our sins,
Lord, who could survive?
But because you forgive
we stand in awe.

I trust in God's word,
I trust in the Lord.
More than sentries for dawn
I watch for the Lord.

More than sentries for dawn
let Israel watch.
The Lord will bring mercy
and grant full pardon.
The Lord will free Israel
from all its sins.

—*Psalm 130*

My soul is bereft of peace; I have forgotten what happiness is; so I say, "Gone is my glory, and all that I had hoped for from the LORD." The thought of my affliction and my homelessness is wormwood and gall! My soul continually thinks of it and is bowed down within me. But this I call to mind and therefore I have hope: The steadfast love of the LORD never ceases, his mercies never come to an end; they are new every morning; great is your faithfulness. "The LORD is my portion," says my soul, "therefore I will hope in him." The LORD is good to those who wait for him, to the soul that seeks him. It is good that one should wait quietly for the salvation of the LORD.

—*Lamentations 3:17–26*

Sometimes I feel like a motherless child,
Sometimes I feel like a motherless child,
Sometimes I feel like a motherless child,
A long way from home,
A long way from home.

Sometimes I feel like I'm almost gone,
Sometimes I feel like I'm almost gone,
Sometimes I feel like I'm almost gone,
A long way from home,
A long way from home.

Sometimes I feel like a moanin' dove,
Sometimes I feel like a moanin' dove,
Sometimes I feel like a moanin' dove,
A long way from home,
A long way from home.

   —*African American spiritual*

PRAYERS FOR INDIVIDUALS

*The prayers in this section are taken from the
Order of Christian Funerals.*

For all who mourn:

Lord our God,
the death of our *brother/sister Name*
recalls our human condition
and the brevity of our lives on earth.
But for those who believe in your love
death is not the end,
nor does it destroy the bonds
that you forge in our lives.
We share the faith of your Son's disciples
and the hope of the children of God.
Bring the light of Christ's resurrection
to this time of testing and pain
as we pray for *Name* and for those
    who love *him/her,*
through Christ our Lord.
Amen.

For a young person:

Lord God,
source and destiny of our lives,
in your loving providence
you gave us *Name*
to grow in wisdom, age and grace.
Now you have called *him/her* to yourself.
We grieve over the loss of one so young
and struggle to understand your purpose.
Draw *him/her* to yourself
and give *him/her* full stature in Christ.
May *he/she* stand with all the angels and saints,
who know your love and praise your saving will.
We ask this through Christ our Lord.
Amen.

For a parent:

God of our ancestors in faith,
by the covenant made on Mount Sinai
you taught your people to strengthen
    the bonds of family
through faith, honor and love.

Look kindly upon *Name,*
a *father/mother* who sought to bind *his/her*
    children to you.
Bring *him/her* one day to our heavenly home
where the saints dwell in blessedness and peace.
We ask this through Christ our Lord.
Amen.

For a wife or husband:

Eternal God,
you made the union of man and woman
a sign of the bond between Christ
    and the church.
Grant mercy and peace to *Name,*
who was united in love with *her husband/*
    his wife.
May the care and devotion of *her/his* life on earth
find a lasting reward in heaven.
Look kindly on *her husband/his wife* and
    family/children
as now they turn to your compassion and love.
Strengthen their faith and lighten their loss.

We ask this through Christ our Lord.
Amen.

For an elderly person:

God of mercy,
look kindly on your servant *Name*
who has set down the burden of *his/her* years.
As *he/she* served you faithfully throughout
    his/her life,
may you give *him/her* the fullness
    of your peace and joy.
We give thanks for the long life of *Name,*
now caught up in your eternal love.
We make our prayer in the name of Jesus who is
    our risen Lord now and for ever.
Amen.

For one who died after a long illness:

Most faithful God,
lively is the courage of those who hope in you.
Your servant *Name* suffered greatly

but placed *his/her* trust in your mercy.
Confident that the petition of those who mourn
pierces the clouds and finds an answer,
we beg you, give rest to *Name.*
Do not remember *his/her* sins
but look upon *his/her* sufferings
and grant *him/her* refreshment, light and peace.
We ask this through Christ our Lord.
Amen.

For one who died suddenly:

Lord,
as we mourn the sudden death
    of our *brother/sister,*
show us the immense power of your goodness
and strengthen our belief
that *Name* has entered into your presence.
We ask this through Christ our Lord.
Amen.

For one who died accidentally or violently:

Lord our God,
you are always faithful and quick to show mercy.
Our *brother/sister Name*
was suddenly *[and violently]* taken from us.
Come swiftly to *his/her* aid,
have mercy on *him/her,*
and comfort *his/her* family and friends
by the power and protection of the cross.
We ask this through Christ our Lord.
Amen.

For one who died by suicide:

God, lover of souls,
you hold dear what you have made
and spare all things, for they are yours.
Look gently on your servant *Name,*
and by the blood of the cross
forgive *his/her* sins and failings.
Remember the faith of those who mourn
and satisfy their longing for that day

when all will be made new again
in Christ, our risen Lord,
who lives and reigns with you for ever and ever.
Amen.

WHEN A CHILD DIES

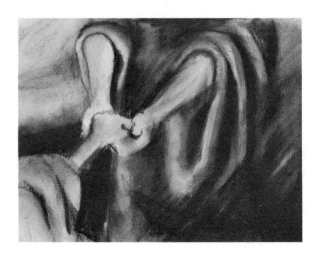

Then little children were being brought to Jesus
in order that he might lay his hands on them
and pray. The disciples spoke sternly to those
who brought them; but Jesus said, "Let the little
children come to me, and do not stop them;
for it is to such as these that the kingdom of
heaven belongs."

—*Matthew 19:13 – 15*

*The prayers in this section are taken from the
Order of Christian Funerals.*

For those who mourn a baptized child:

Lord of all gentleness,
surround us with your care
and comfort us in our sorrow,
for we grieve at the loss of this [little] child.
As you washed *Name* in the waters of baptism
and welcomed *him/her* into the life of heaven,
so call us one day
to be united with *him/her*

and share for ever the joy of your kingdom.
We ask this through Christ our Lord.
Amen.

For those who mourn a child who died before baptism:

O Lord, whose ways are beyond understanding,
listen to the prayers of your faithful people:
that those weighed down by grief
at the loss of this [little] child
may find reassurance in your infinite goodness.
We ask this through Christ our Lord.
Amen.

For those who mourn a stillborn child:

Lord God,
ever caring and gentle,
we commit to your love this little one,
quickened to life for so short a time.
Enfold *him/her* in eternal life.
We pray for *his/her* parents

who are saddened by the loss of their child.
Give them courage
and help them in their pain and grief.
May they all meet one day
in the joy and peace of your kingdom.
We ask this through Christ our Lord.
Amen.

For the child:

To you, O Lord,
we humbly entrust this child,
so precious in your sight.
Take *him/her* into your arms
and welcome *him/her* into paradise,
where there will be no sorrow,
 no weeping nor pain,
but the fullness of peace and joy
with your Son and the Holy Spirit
for ever and ever.
Amen.

ON THE ANNIVERSARY
OF DEATH

The souls of the righteous are in the hand of God, and no torment will ever touch them. In the eyes of the foolish they seem to have died, and their departure was thought to be a disaster, and their going from us to be their destruction; but they are at peace. For though in the sight of others they were punished, their hope is full of immortality. Having been disciplined a little, they will receive great good, because God tested them and found them worthy of himself; like gold in the furnace he tried them, and like a sacrificial burnt offering he accepted them. In the time of their visitation they will shine forth and will run like sparks through the stubble. The faithful will abide with God in love, because grace and mercy are upon his holy ones, and he watches over his elect.

—*Wisdom 3:1 – 7, 9b*

Into your hands, O Lord,
we humbly entrust our *brother/sister Name.*

In this life you embraced *him/her*
  with your tender love;
deliver *him/her* now from every evil
and bid *him/her* enter eternal rest.

The old order has passed away:
welcome *him/her* then into paradise,
where there will be no sorrow,
  no weeping nor pain,
but the fullness of peace and joy
with your Son and the Holy Spirit
for ever and ever.
Amen.

— *Order of Christian Funerals*

I'll be singing up there,
I'll be singing up there,
Oh! come on up to bright glory,
I'll be singing up there.

  If you miss me singing down here,
  If you miss me singing down here,
  Oh, come on up to bright glory,
  You'll find me singing up there.

If you miss me praying down here . . .
If you miss me walking down here . . .
If you miss me shouting down here . . .

—*African American spiritual*

Give rest, O Christ,
  to your servant with your saints:
  where sorrow and pain are no more;
  neither sighing, but life everlasting.
You only are immortal,
  the creator and maker of humankind:
  and we are mortal, formed of the earth,
  and unto earth shall we return:
  for so you did ordain,
  when thou created me, saying,
  "Dust you are, and unto dust shall you return."
All we go down to the dust;
  and weeping over the grave,
  we make our song:
  Alleluia, alleluia, alleluia.

—*Contakion of the Departed from the Orthodox liturgy*

VISITING THE CEMETERY

It is good — not morbid or macabre — for Christians to visit the cemetery, especially in November. Remember what the Bible tells us: God planted a garden and made our first parents from the dust of the earth. Adam and Eve's sin exiled them from Eden, and ever since then human beings have longed for the garden of paradise. His saving passion completed, Jesus was buried in a new tomb in a garden, forever making graves and graveyards holy places. And when Magdalene spotted the Risen Lord at dawn, she thought he was the gardener! The cemetery reminds us of the Bible's gardens.

We show great respect for the remains of the dead — committing the body to mother earth or father fire — because while living, the body of the baptized, anointed one was a temple of the Holy Spirit. So we decorate the graves of our loved ones who have died to remember and to respect them.

Read this scripture before leaving for the cemetery:
On the first day of the week, at early dawn,
they came to the tomb, taking the spices that they
had prepared. They found the stone rolled
away from the tomb, but when they went in, they
did not find the body. While they were per-
plexed about this, suddenly two men in dazzling
clothes stood beside them. The women were
terrified and bowed their faces to the ground,
but the men said to them, "Why do you look for
the living among the dead? He is not here
but has risen. Remember how he told you, while
he was still in Galilee, that the Son of Man must
be handed over to sinners, and be crucified,
and on the third day rise again." Then they
remembered his words.

—*Luke 24:1–8*

The care bestowed upon the burial of the
body is no aid to salvation. It is merely an act of
humanity regulated by affection. It is most
proper that one should care for the corpse of a

neighbor when that neighbor has died. If
these offices are paid to the dead, even by those
who do not believe in the resurrection of the
body, how much more should they be paid
by those who do believe in the resurrection on
the last day? Thus these duties toward a body,
which although dead is destined to rise again and
to live throughout eternity, are in a way a testi-
mony of faith in that belief.

—*St. Augustine*

O God,
by whose mercy the faithful departed find rest,
send your holy angel to watch over this grave.
We ask this through Christ our Lord.

—*Catholic Household Blessings and Prayers*

In sure and certain hope of the resurrection
to eternal life
through our Lord Jesus Christ,

we commend to Almighty God our *brother/*
sister Name,
and we commit *his/her* body to the ground:
earth to earth, ashes to ashes, dust to dust.

The Lord bless *him/her* and keep *him/her,*
the Lord make his face to shine upon *him/her*
and be gracious to *him/her,*
the Lord lift up his countenance upon *him/her*
and give *him/her* peace.

— *Book of Common Prayer*

This body sleeps in dust
Immortal joys await the host
In perfect beauty may it rise
When Gabriel's trumpet shakes the skies.

— *Epitaph on a tombstone in Long Island, New York*

The hand of the LORD came upon me, and
he brought me out by the spirit of the LORD and
set me down in the middle of a valley; it was full
of bones. He led me all around them; there were

many lying in the valley, and they were very dry. The LORD said to me, "Mortal, can these bones live?" I answered, "O Lord GOD, you know." Then he said to me, "Prophesy to these bones, and say to them: O dry bones, hear the word of the LORD. Thus says the Lord GOD: I am going to open your graves and bring you up from your graves, O my people; and I will bring you back to the land of Israel. And you shall know that I am the LORD, when I open your graves and bring you up from your graves, O my people. I will put my spirit within you, and you shall live, and I will place you on your own soil; then you shall know that I, the LORD, have spoken and will act."

— *Ezekiel 37:1–4, 12–14*

Sing this song to any common meter tune, such as "O God, our help in ages past" or "Land of rest."

Jerusalem, my happy home,
    when shall I with you be?

When shall my sorrows have an end?
　　Your joys when shall I see?

Your saints are crowned with glory great;
　　they see God face to face.
They triumph still, they still rejoice:
　　in that most holy place.

Jerusalem, Jerusalem, God grant that I may see
Your endless joy and of the same partaker ever be!

　—*Joseph Bromehead*

O God this hour revives in us memories of loved
ones who are no more. What happiness we
shared when they walked among us! What joy,
when, loving and loved, we lived our lives
together!

Their memory is a blessing forever.

Months or years may have passed, yet we feel
near to them. Our hearts yearn for them.
Though the bitter grief has softened, a duller
pain abides, for the place where once they stood

is empty now forever. The links of life are broken. But the links of love and longing cannot break.

Their souls are bound up with ours forever.

We see them now with the eye of memory, their faults forgiven, their virtues grown larger. So does goodness live and weakness fade from sight. We remember them with gratitude and bless their names.

Their memory is a blessing forever.

And we remember as well the men and women who but yesterday were part of our congregation and community. To all who cared for us and labored for the well-being of our people and of humanity we pay tribute. May we prove worthy of carrying on the tradition of our people and our faith, for now the task is ours.

Their souls are bound up with ours forever.

We think, too, of the whole household of Israel and its martyrs. The tragedy of our own age is still a fresh wound within us. And we recall how often in ages past our people walked through the flames of the furnace. Merciful God, let the memory never fade of the faithful and upright of our people who have given their lives to hallow your name. Even in death they continue to speak to us of faith and courage. They rest in nameless graves, but their deeds endure, and their sacrifices will not be forgotten. Their souls are bound up in the bond of eternal life. No evil shall touch them; they are at peace.

We will remember and never forget them.

In gratitude for all the blessings our loved ones, our friends, our teachers, and the martyrs of our people have brought to us, to our people, and to humanity, we dedicate ourselves anew to the sacred faith for which they lived and died and to the tasks they have bequeathed to us. Let

them be remembered for blessing, O God,
together with the righteous of all peoples, and
let us say:

Amen.

Silent remembrance.

May God remember forever my dear ones,
Names, who have gone to their eternal rest. May
they be at one with the One who is life eternal.
May the beauty of their lives shine for evermore,
and may my life always bring honor to their
memory.

—*Central Conference of American Rabbis*

O Lord Jesus Christ, King of glory, deliver the
souls of all the faithful departed from the pains
of hell and from the deep pit: Deliver them from
the lion's mouth, that hell may not swallow
them up, and may they not fall into darkness.
May your holy standard-bearer Michael lead

them into the holy light which you promised to Abraham and to his seed.

— *Missal of Pius V*

We do not want you to be uninformed, brothers and sisters, about those who have died, so that you may not grieve as others do who have no hope. For since we believe that Jesus died and rose again, even so, through Jesus, God will bring with him those who have died. For this we declare to you by the word of the Lord, that we who are alive, who are left until the coming of the Lord, will by no means precede those who have died. For the Lord himself, with a cry of command, with the archangel's call and with the sound of God's trumpet, will descend from heaven, and the dead in Christ will rise first. Then we who are alive, who are left, will be caught up in the clouds together with them to meet the Lord in the air; and so we will be with the

Lord forever. Therefore encourage one another
with these words.

— *1 Thessalonians 4:13 – 18*

Eternal rest grant unto *Name,* O Lord,
and let perpetual light shine upon *him/her.*
May *Name* rest in peace.
May *Name's* soul and the souls of all the faithful
      departed,
through the mercy of God, rest in peace. Amen.